Man on the Moon

The Story of Neil A...

Christine
Butterworth

Contents

OXFORD
UNIVERSITY PRESS

OXFORD
UNIVERSITY PRESS

Great Clarendon Street, Oxford OX2 6DP

Oxford University Press is a department of the University of Oxford.
It furthers the University's objective of excellence in research, scholarship,
and education by publishing worldwide in

Oxford New York

Auckland Bangkok Buenos Aires Cape Town Chennai
Dar es Salaam Delhi Hong Kong Istanbul Karachi Kolkata
Kuala Lumpur Madrid Melbourne Mexico City Mumbai Nairobi
São Paulo Shanghai Taipei Tokyo Toronto

Oxford is a registered trade mark of Oxford University Press
in the UK and in certain other countries

British Library Cataloguing in Publication Data

Data available

ISBN 0 19 919541 2

10 9 8 7 6 5 4

True Stories Pack 2 (one of each title) ISBN 0 19 919544 7
True Stories Pack 2 Class Pack (six of each title) ISBN 0 19 919545 5

Acknowledgements

The publisher would like to thank the following for permission
to reproduce photographs:

Associated Press/Peter Cosgrove: p 29; Corbis: p 6; Corbis/Bettmann: p 20;
NASA: pp 3 (*both*), 7, 9, 10, 12, 19, 25.

Front cover background artwork: NASA
Inset photo: NASA
Back cover: NASA

Illustrations are by Kevin Hopgood
Rocket artwork is by David Russell

Printed in Great Britain by Ashford Colour Press, Gosport, Hants

In 1969 the United States of America sent three men to the Moon.

Their spacecraft was called *Apollo 11*, and their leader was a man called Neil Armstrong.

Neil's dream had always been to go to the Moon. This is the story of how he got there.

Neil Armstrong, born August 5th 1930 in Ohio, USA

Chapter 1

Mad About Flying

As a boy Neil Armstrong was mad about planes. He watched planes at Cleveland airfield when he was two. At six he went up in a plane called the *Tin Goose*.

He had flying lessons when he was still at school, and he got his pilot's **licence** when he was just 16.

In 1950 Neil joined the Navy to fly planes in the **Korean War**. He flew 78 missions, escaping danger even when his plane was damaged.

His skill and bravery earned him three medals, and after the war he went back to finish his studies in **aeronautics**.

Race to the moon

Neil's studies ended just as the space race began.

The Russians sent a **sputnik** (**satellite**) into space in 1957, followed three years later by Yuri Gagarin, the first **cosmonaut**.

The American government felt they had to catch up, and President Kennedy promised that America would put a man on the moon by 1970.

A Russian stamp showing Yuri Gagarin

Neil as a test pilot

This was just what Neil wanted to hear.

"Space is where I intend to go," Neil said, in 1962.

At that time he was a **test pilot** for **NASA**, taking the X-15 rocket plane to the edge of space – 63,200 metres up – and flying at five times the speed of sound.

Getting to the Moon was Neil's goal, and his wife and friends knew that this quiet but determined man usually got where he wanted to go.

He joined the astronaut training programme, spending many hours in a model **cockpit**, learning how to control a spacecraft.

He was spun at very high speeds (like sitting in a **supersonic** roller-coaster) to see how he would cope with being sent up into space in a rocket.

Neil's astronaut training was tough.

His trainers made him face mock disasters to see how he could cope with them.

Neil's cool nerve carried him through.

In 1969 Neil achieved his goal. He was to lead the *Apollo 11* mission: the rocket that was to land on the Moon.

Buzz Aldrin and Michael Collins were to go with him, and they trained for six months, flying models of the spacecraft.

By July everything was ready.

The three astronauts on launch day

Record of the Moon Mission

16th July 1969 — launch day

4.15 a.m. (Houston time)

Neil gets up, eats a steak-and-eggs breakfast.

6.00 a.m.

The crew get into their space suits and are driven out to the 110 metres-high *Saturn* rocket on the launch pad.

As watchers cheer, the three men enter the rocket. They now have a three-hour wait as the control systems are checked.

The Washington Post

LIFT OFF

9.32 a.m.

Saturn's rockets fire. With a roar, flames gush from its base. Slowly, it lifts, then shoots up into the blue sky. Forty seconds later it is travelling faster than the speed of sound.

Lift-off!

9.35 a.m.

The first stage rocket is detached from the spacecraft.

9.41 a.m.

The second stage rocket falls away. The third stage rocket takes the craft out of the Earth's atmosphere and into **orbit** 184 kilometres above the Earth.

Less than three hours later the rocket fires again, launching the ship towards the Moon at a speed of 38,800 kilometres per hour.

The complete *Apollo 11* spacecraft

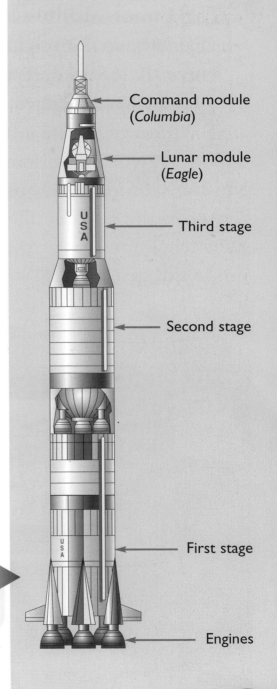

Command module (*Columbia*)

Lunar module (*Eagle*)

Third stage

Second stage

First stage

Engines

The **Lunar Module** and the Command and Service Modules are flying alone now.

Inside the cabin everything is weightless, and the men (and all other objects!) float around unless they are fixed down.

The crew is in constant two-way contact with Mission Control in **Houston**.

Across the Earth, millions of people crowd round their televisions to see pictures sent back from inside the spacecraft.

18th July [Midnight]

The ship is travelling towards the Moon.

Three days after leaving Earth the rocket motors fire twice, to change course and bring *Apollo* into the Moon's orbit.

20th July Noon

It is the fourth day of the mission, and the final stage of the journey has begun. It is time for the Lunar Module (called *Eagle*) to separate from the Command Module. Left alone in the Command Module, Michael Collins pushes the button to release the *Eagle*.

"There you go! You guys take care," he calls to Neil and Buzz Aldrin who are in the *Eagle*.

Once they are free of the main craft, Neil sends the *Eagle* into a slow spin.

"The *Eagle* has wings!" he calls out to Mission control.

He takes the *Eagle* down at 21 metres per second. He scans the **craters** and dust plains of the Moon's surface below, searching for a safe landing site.

Chapter 4

"The *Eagle* has Landed"

At 300 metres Neil sees they are heading for huge boulders, and he takes over from the computer, flying the Module himself.

The final 60 metres are the most dangerous. The Module is going so fast that Neil must land, even if things go wrong. Astronauts call this "the dead man's curve".

"I'm going right over a crater – I've got to get further over," Neil says.

Down on Earth in Mission Control, people are holding their breath. Neil must land before the fuel runs out. Then, with 20 seconds of fuel left, they hear his voice.

"Houston, Tranquility Base here. The *Eagle* has landed."

Cheers for Neil and his team at Mission Control

Neil has landed the Lunar Module on a flat plain. Craters and boulders can be seen clearly where the Sun's bright light falls on the Moon. There is just black space beyond the horizon. No stars are visible in the black sky, just the blue Earth in the distance.

"It's big, bright and beautiful."
Neil Armstrong

The astronauts are supposed to rest, but they are too excited to sleep. They seal their space suits and Neil crawls out through the tiny hatch.

Back on Earth, 600 million people watch him slowly climb down the ladder and step onto the Moon.

"That's one small step for Man, one giant leap for Mankind," Neil says.

Neil walks slowly and stiffly. The Moon's **gravity** is so weak that Neil finds it hard to walk normally.

Buzz joins him, and for over two hours they walk on the dusty surface of the Moon.

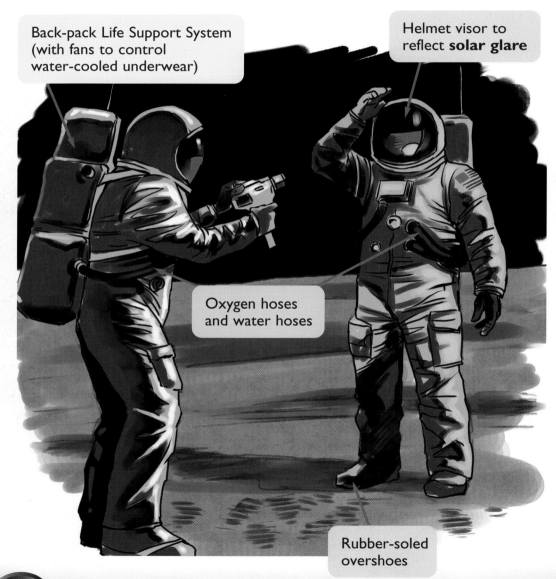

Back-pack Life Support System (with fans to control water-cooled underwear)

Helmet visor to reflect **solar glare**

Oxygen hoses and water hoses

Rubber-soled overshoes

The Moon's light brown surface curves away to the black horizon.

As the astronauts walk they leave sharp-edged footprints in the dust that may stay there for a billion years.

One fifth of the world's population watch their ghostly, floating figures on television – the biggest audience for any event in history.

President Nixon congratulates them by telephone. "It's a great honour for us to be here," Neil replies. He remembers the years of work that scientists, **engineers** and pilots have given to make this great event happen.

There is still scientific work to be done before the men leave.

Neil and Buzz set up one experiment to detect lunar earthquakes, and another to measure exactly their distance from the Earth.

Then they collect samples of moon rock, but they are running out of time.

"The Moon has a stark beauty all its own." *Neil Armstrong*

Chapter 5

Return to Earth

It is time to leave. They return to the *Eagle* and fill the cabin with oxygen.

As they take off their helmets, the moon dust on their suits smells like wet ashes. They try to sleep but lie shivering in the cramped, cold Module.

It is a relief when the time comes to take off.

Eagle's Landing Module is left on the Moon; the rockets fire, and three hours later they join up with Michael Collins and the Command Module. Their return to Earth will take three days.

In the last stage, the Command Module glows red-hot as it takes a zigzag course down through the Earth's atmosphere.

Only an hour after splashing down in the Pacific Ocean, the astronauts are on their way home, still inside the Module.

Their trip is not over yet; they must spend the next 21 days in **quarantine**, until scientists can be sure that they have not brought any lunar germs back with them.

When the trip is finally over, the crew are world heroes. They visit 25 countries and are awarded medals and honours wherever they go.

Neil Armstrong, the man who went to the Moon, has been happy to stay in Ohio ever since he came back down to Earth.

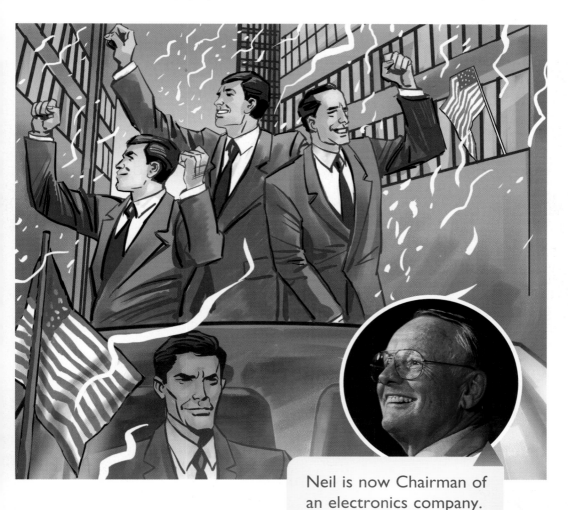

Neil is now Chairman of an electronics company.

Glossary

aeronautics   the study of aircraft and flying

astronaut   someone who travels in a spacecraft

cockpit   the place in which the pilot sits and controls an aircraft or spacecraft

cosmonaut   someone who travels in a spacecraft

crater   a dip, or hole in the ground, left after a rock has hit the surface

engineer   someone who designs and builds engines or machines

gravity   the force that pulls everything down to the surface of the Earth, or the Moon

Houston   the site of the NASA Space Centre in Texas, USA

Korean War   the war between North and South Korea from 1950–53

licence   an official document that allows someone to drive a car, or fly a plane

Lunar Module   the part of a spacecraft that travels to the Moon

NASA   the National Aeronautics and Space Administration of the USA

orbit   the path taken by something moving round a planet in space

quarantine   the time a person has to spend alone, to stop a disease from spreading

satellite   something that is sent out to orbit the Earth, or another planet, to collect information

solar glare   brightness from the Sun

sputnik   the name given to the first Russian satellite sent into space

supersonic   faster than the speed of sound

test pilot   a pilot who tests new kinds of aircraft

Index